INTERNATIONAL

"The Book That Lies Flat"
— *User Friendly Binding* —

This title has been bound using state-of-the-art **OtaBind®** technology.

- The spine is 3-5 times stronger than conventional perfect binding
- The book lies open flat, regardless of the page being read
- The spine floats freely and remains crease-free even with repeated use

We are pleased to be able to bring this new technology to our customers.

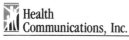

Health Communications, Inc.

3201 S.W. 15th Street
Deerfield Beach, FL 33442-8190
(305) 360-0909

The Netherlands

Other Books In This Series Are:

Health Communications, Inc.
3201 S.W. 15th Street
Deerfield Beach, FL 33442-8190
Phone: (800) 851-9100

ANGRY? DO YOU MIND
IF I SCREAM?

How To Handle Your Anger

Devon Weber

Health Communications, Inc.
Deerfield Beach, Florida

Devon Weber
Inner Dynamics
Dayton, Ohio

© 1991 Devon Weber
ISBN 1-55874-157-7

Publisher: Health Communications, Inc.
          3201 S.W. 15th Street
          Deerfield Beach, Florida 33442-8190

ACKNOWLEDGMENTS

I would like to thank Gay Taylor Hunger for discovering my talents while appearing on the Sally Jessy Raphael Show with me, and for inspiring me to write this book. Her loving support and encouragement make it possible for me to journey into the world of writing. I am also grateful to my agent, John Hunger, who made it happen. He took a dream of mine and turned it into a reality. Special appreciation is also due to Mary Ann Townsend for her input on body signals. Thank you Wendy Tardiff, for your help in typing and for making writing this book fun. My sincere thanks to Terri Cain for her creativity in helping me capture the emotions of my inner child. A heartfelt thanks to Darlene Olsen, who is by my side during my darkest hours. To Zig Ziglar, whose gentle guidance enabled me to open up to my spiritual self and trust in God's love. And to Rosita Perez, who believed in me before I could believe in myself.

DEDICATED

To my husband Flemming,
who had the courage to stand up
to my anger, and the patience
to teach me how to love.

As a mental health therapist, I would like to share the following case study with you. I was working with Mary, a 51-year-old woman who was attending an incest survivors group, who noticed that whenever Mary was talking about something painful, she would laugh. I gently confronted her about her laughter, by helping her see that what she was talking about was not funny but painful. Mary started to sob.

She said she wasn't even aware of her laughter. She remembered exactly when her behavior began. Mary said that when she was a very young girl, her mother would beat her with a hair brush and scream, "Until you stop that crying, I'm not going to stop hitting you."

Poor little Mary learned that she could not cry when things hurt her. She knew at a very young age that crying was wrong. She protected herself by laughing her pain away.

In the group that day, it wasn't the adult Mary in the room. It was the little Mary of many, many years ago. With the safety and support of the group, Mary learned to respond to pain appropriately.

This is the message I want you to hear: Awareness is your key to change. Until it was brought to Mary's attention, how could she change a behavior she didn't know existed?

What awareness are you beginning to gain insight into? What action do you want to take? Take a moment to jot down your first thoughts.

_____

_____

_____

_____

_____

The following exercise will teach you about yourself, helping you become aware of your angry side. Awareness is your key to a productive change.

As you read you will begin to want to change your unhealthy angry behavior. As you complete the exercises, you will see what changes you want to make. The workbook is structured to help you focus your energies toward taking healthy action.

Uncovery/ Recovery

So many adults who come from dysfunctional backgrounds confuse recovery with absence of pain. In my opinion recovery means taking the journey into the soul to *uncover* and connect with your original pain feelings. The only way to find peace is to search for the wounded child within who will validate you with truth. The answers are always within your reach.

Addicts who no longer drink or take drugs may think they are recovered because they have been able to change a destructive behavior. I believe that until they know why they masked their pain in the first place, cathartic healing does not occur. They stop acting out their pain in addictive behaviors, abusive relationships or co-dependency, only to find themselves obsessed in other areas. They become overly dependent and act out their neediness by reading every self-help book on the market or attending every AA, ACoA or CoDA meeting offered. These are the people who experience severe anxiety if they miss one support group. They may have stopped abusing themselves in one area, but they still have not found inner peace.

By uncovering and taking the journey inward to discover their true source of pain, they can learn to validate themselves and find comfort.

Uncover To Discover To Recover

One of my clients, Debbie, is a nurse. She came to me for help for her addiction to drugs. She had been arrested for writing illegal prescriptions to get drugs to support her habit. Debbie was experiencing extreme anxiety, fearing that she would lose her license to practice nursing. She also feared going to prison because this was her second offense with drugs.

During therapy I could clearly see that Debbie was not in touch with her childhood experiences. I suspected that she had been abused as a child and that she was acting out her pain by setting herself up to fail in her adult life.

We began doing original pain work, using visualizations to regress Debbie to her past. She was able to embrace her wounded inner child who had been severely abused and incested. She began the grieving process. As a child she had never been safe enough to express her pain. Now she began to free herself from the shame she had been hiding since childhood. She finally became aware of why she had needed to take drugs in the first place.

Debbie had been hospitalized several times in the past because of her addiction. The treatment centers she had attended focused on an intellectual understanding of her behavior without uncovering the emotional feelings that led to her drug abuse.

Debbie would find short-term relief only to return to drugs to medicate her pain. Her wounded child was never validated, so Debbie needed to hide from the truth. Recovery means uncovering first.

Today Debbie works with troubled teens and also speaks about drugs and drug abuse on a national level. Debbie's journey inward helped her find a meaningful purpose for her life. She attends meetings on a regular basis to get support and no longer fears going back to using drugs.

Reading self-help books and attending meetings are excellent ways to find support. AA, CoDA and ACoA meetings are highly recommended by myself and many other helping professionals. However, until you walk the walk by exploring the feelings that you have locked inside and connect with your inner child, you will find no peace.

If you experience feelings as you read about my story or the stories of others, be careful not to feel in the name of someone else's pain. You really cannot feel someone else's pain. You can only feel the emotions that are inside you. Why not begin your recovery by going into your own feelings and *uncovering* the child in you? Avoid comparing. If you find yourself saying, "Poor Devon, she had it worse than me," remember: If hurt is in your gut, it is every bit as painful as anything I went through. By comparing, you may be minimizing your own pain. Our stories may be different, yet many of the dynamics may be the same.

THE MAKING OF AN ANGRY CHILD

Like any other six year old, she needed her daddy to protect her, to keep her safe from the darkness and monsters of the night.

The small house where her dad lived belonged to his parents, as did the many wooded acres that kept it secluded from the lights of the city and the eyes and ears of the city dwellers. This particular weekend the woods seemed more closed in, darker and more menacing than usual. Even as they approached the door, fear reigned over her.

To the left of the door was the window where her dad had carefully centered the rollaway bed on which she was to sleep. As she looked at the window, fear pounded at her chest.

Although daylight had long since faded to darkness, she didn't want to go to bed. She was so afraid of the dark. She didn't want to be alone.

"Daddy, will you stay with me? I'm afraid of the dark," she told him. "I don't want to sleep down here by myself."

He glanced over his shoulder through the window at the darkness beyond, and with that look her dad always had, turned back to her. "There's nothing out there at night that isn't there in the daylight. You're acting like a big baby!" he scolded.

"Could you please just close the curtain then?" she begged.

His answer was quick and stabbing. "No," he said coldly and matter of factly, "but I will lock the door."

The dead bolt snapped locked, but she felt more trapped than protected. Her insides shook with fear as her dad reached for the light switch. She begged him, "Daddy, please don't turn out the light. Don't make me sleep down here alone. Please, Daddy. Please!"

Without another word he turned off the light and headed for the stairs. As he reached the top, the only remaining light clicked out.

She was alone with the darkness, a bolted door, an open curtain and an immobilizing fear.

For a long time she lay still, unable to sleep and too frightened to cry. Then it happened. Just as she feared it would, it happened. Screaming monster noises outside, moving nearer and nearer to the house. Abruptly the noises ceased. Except for the chirping of crickets and her battering heart, the night was once again quiet. She lay deathly still in the dark, afraid even to breathe. *Where was that monster?*

Moments later came the startling, pounding monster noises at the door. Then she saw it. In the window before her that loathsome monster, in an enraged fury, was bellowing hideous sounds and thrashing and flailing its arms. It moved from the window to the door . . . and back . . . and back. Still frozen with fear, she was unable to move. Then with one furious blow, the very door her dad had bolted closed was broken to pieces and she was face to face with the monster. It lunged toward her, grabbing her throat, viciously strangling her. Her head, helpless against the forces, jerked in violent circles.

She couldn't cry out, for the beast was choking the very life from her body. At last just one tiny, helpless cry as the horrid demon released her throat and hurled her back against the bed. Swaggering back, the monster removed from his face a nylon stocking. My God — it was her daddy!

"You Mamma's baby," he scoffed. "It's only your daddy."

Her insides trembled. Her mind and body had been traumatized.

"Please, Daddy, can I sleep with you now?" she pleaded wearily. Complacently, he agreed.

The moon shone through the remnants of the shattered door, casting eerie reflections on the fireplace and dimly lighting the gallery of naked women her dad had drawn on the walls leading to his bedroom. With each sound of his feet on the creaky wooden stairs, she grew angrier and more defiant. She took a breath, breathing deep into her memory the dark, musty smell of the cottage. "All right," she decided, "go ahead — be that way — play your game, but I'm not going to play with Peter tonight."

She woke the next morning from a series of short, restless catnaps, frightened of the emotion she had felt the night before, and angry toward her dad for what he had done to her.

To see him was to be reminded of the evil that had engulfed his usually handsome face. The evil had filtered down through his fingertips, forming a death grip on her throat. Each time he spoke, his lips hinted at the familiar lines of that sadistic smile. And his voice — oh, that voice — a chilling reminder of the screeching, screaming monster noises outside her door. "But I won't think about that right now," she told herself.

She had stayed emotionally distant and out of anxiety for what he might do kept her angry feelings silently locked away.

But the silence she was using for self-preservation became the weapon by which her purpose was betrayed. Her dad realized that what he was sensing through the silence was not the fear that had given him power last night, but her rage! He feared losing control, and now he was threatened by her!

It was in an attempt to regain control that he threatened to spank her. His threat only fueled the intensity of the anger she already felt.

"You're not my dad," she screamed at him. "You don't live with me! I don't see you that much, and you're not going to spank me!"

Indirectly she was expressing the rage she was feeling over what he had done to her. In doing so she became the stronger one and took charge. Her control frightened him. He knew she was angry and he knew why.

The fact that she was angry and hurting did not disturb him. He didn't care. What bothered him was that his "power tool" (her fear) was gone, having been replaced with the strength of will and determination born of her anger. He had lost control. If he couldn't dominate and terrorize her, he wanted nothing to do with her. He could see that she was truly the stronger one.

He shot her a look that said unmistakably, "You're not worth my time. You're just not that important to me." It was a look that made her next breath hurt. She moved away, barely noticed.

He collected her few belongings and placed them near the door. Why? She didn't know. But as always, she was guided by her instincts. Her actions were merely reactions to the actions of others. She crouched motionlessly in the shadows of the massive stone fireplace. In fearful silence and confusion she watched him, knowing she dare not make an utterance that might give away the secret suspicions swarming in her head. "What if Daddy knows I'm angry with him? What if he knows why?" she wondered. "Will he try to hurt me again?" A lump caught in her throat, a burning began in her nose. Her chin quivered at the thought. Then came a thought even more frightening: "What if Daddy doesn't love me anymore? And all because I got angry. What then? Oh, no. What then?" She heaved a silent sigh, but never a tear, never a sound.

A cab pulled up outside. Her dad made no effort to explain. He simply moved her things outside and ushered her out behind them.

She looked out at the cab, then hesitantly back over her shoulder. The door was closed, her dad was gone. Through the battered door she caught a glimpse of him moving away up the stairs. There was nothing wrong for him, only for her. She was bad and now she was being punished. Her father never came for her again.

For 27 years she had blocked the memory of what happened to her in the cottage that night, turning all the anger and rage in on herself. I know this story very well because the scared little girl in the cottage was me.

My father's rejection caused me to turn my anger and rage in on myself. No matter what my father had done to me, I was still a helpless little girl who needed her daddy to protect her. To survive, I had learned that expressing anger meant rejection. Because I had suppressed the terror of that night, I experienced severe panic attacks throughout my childhood and adult life, I acted out my pain in abusive relationships. Until I recognized the patterns in my life and began tracing my anger, linking it to the little girl, I found no freedom.

I am able to share this story because I am now strong enough that I no longer feel shame. I want you to see that the messages we receive as children can profoundly affect our lives as adults. If you feel pain in the name of my story, please understand that you cannot feel someone else's pain. You can only feel the pain in your own gut. Breathe into the pain, for this is how you begin to find your own inner truth.

If your thoughts are that your story is not as bad as mine or is worse than mine, let me remind you that you cannot compare pain. What hurts inside of you is as significant as anything that has hurt me.

You only become as sick as the secrets you keep. Your healing begins when you confront those secrets, clean those skeletons out of your closet and break the pattern of secrets.

For the adult child awareness can often be the hardest part of the recovery process because your conscious mind is blocked from the truth. For this reason it is crucial to have supportive, strong people around you as you begin your anger work.

As you begin working through the exercises, you may not be aware of your history or where your anger is coming from. For many years I had no idea that I had abuse issues. Without loving support (books, tapes, workshops or your own therapist), the only way you can become aware is by recognizing patterns in your life. It took several marriages for me to realize, "Gee, I have problems with relationships." If you have blocked or denied your pain, the message to you is that as a little one, you were not safe enough to feel it. If you do not have safe support in your adult life, your original pain will come out indirectly . . . on yourself or others.

When you are working your anger out in the name of a relationship, the storyline may be totally different from the stories you remember as a child. But I assure you, the dynamics will be the same. This means that the way you end up feeling as a result of your relationship is how the child in you felt within the family. Your anger can become the missing link that allows you to heal. When you spend your life dreaming about the person you would like to be or the person you would like to be with, you waste the person you are.

As survivors of dysfunctional families, our lives become so complicated and blocked up that it is often the most simple affirmation that gives us insight. An affirmation that I learned not too many years ago is, "Do the thing you fear the most, and that will be the end of fear." I have based major changes on this affirmation.

LISTING YOUR SUPPORT SOURCES

Just being able to ask for support is a major sign of recovery. What about you? Can you reach out? Who's there for you? If you're waiting to be totally secure to take a risk, you'll be waiting a lifetime.

Make a list of the people or places in your life that are supportive.

Name or Place	How do you feel supported by this person or place?
_____	_____
_____	_____
_____	_____

Now list the people or places that are negative in your life. What action do you need to take?

Negative	Action
_____	_____
_____	_____
_____	_____

How to determine if support is healthy.

- Person/place focuses on strengths, not weaknesses.
- You feel good around this person/place.
- Person/place provides you with hope.

People are social beings. We need one another for survival.

CONNECTING WITH THE CHILD WITHIN

Using the opposite hand you usually write with, make a list of what you needed as a child but didn't get. Now go back to your dominant writing hand and list how the wounded child would feel if he/she didn't get these things.

Example:

What child needed	How wounded child would feel
• to be safe	• frightened
• to be protected	• helpless, hopeless

What you needed	How you would feel
_____	_____
_____	_____

Make a list of how you end up feeling within intimate relationships. Can you find your wounded child acting out in your adult relationships?

_____

_____

_____

_____

WRITING A LOVE LETTER TO YOUR INNER CHILD

On a separate sheet of paper, write a love letter to your inner child. Use as much space as you need.

A Message Of Hope: A Survivor's Story

My healing has come from my own personal struggle as a victim of childhood sexual abuse and torture. I was conceived out of anger, born under angry circumstances and have been around conflict and violence almost my entire life. My father was a violent sexual psychopath. His alcoholism brought out a mental disorder called paranoid schizophrenia. My mother was cold, emotionally dead and unavailable for me. Because of the circumstances surrounding my birth, she also took her anger out on me. By the time I was one year old I had already learned some devastating messages about anger. By the time I was 15 I was in knock-down, drag-out relationships, trying to work out through abuse my issues with males. My journey toward recovery has been long and difficult, involving many losses. I call this a journey from the world of darkness into the world of light.

As a survivor of childhood sexual abuse and incest, it took multiple marriages, physical illness and enough pain and trauma to cause me to have an emotional breakdown before I realized I had a problem. As a result of an abusive marriage, at age 31 I lost custody of my three small children and ended up homeless, living in the streets to survive. It took this kind of trauma to break down the inappropriate defenses that I developed as a child. In my adult life I had to set myself up for so much pain I would hit rock bottom and be stripped of my identity before I could let down my defenses. There was only one choice left: I had to feel. Finally I *really* had to feel my pain.

I began to visit a dark space within my soul, feeling the same pain, fear and darkness that was all too familiar. Here I experienced a sense of my helplessness and hopelessness. This was the hardest part of the journey. Uncovering the missing link to my suffering, I found the frightened child within me. I began to understand that the helplessness I felt in my childhood was the same helplessness I was setting up in my adult life. With only a molecule of energy to draw from, I chose to fight for freedom. Painfully, slowly, I began to find hope by understanding and nurturing the vulnerable child within. The innocent little one finally knew I would love and protect her.

For so long my life had seemed like a jigsaw puzzle. Yet I had no idea how the pieces fit together. Nowhere to go, no one to turn to — except myself. No one could hear my pain. Only me. I began to realize that I wasn't really alone. *I was there with me.* It was with this inner knowledge and connection that I began to find and trust the lovingness in me. My surviving child was crying out for peace. I embraced a part of me I had not felt, the loving, hurting child — letting her know

I heard her desperate cry. She would never be alone again.

Sometimes the puzzle of my life is still incomplete. Many pieces are still out of place. I am beginning to see the big picture, and it looks and feels good to me. I no longer jigsaw, I journey. For the most part I choose the paths I wish to take. Once in a while the universe forces me down paths I don't wish to walk. But even during those times when I'm afraid of myself or afraid of others, my determined child reminds me that I have choices and I'm never really alone. Now that I have a loving connection with myself, I have so many people who support me even during my darkest hours.

I now know that my pain is my existence, that I will never be totally pain-free. I choose to accept this reality. This is the choice that sets me free.

During these times when I do experience pain, I'm not immobilized with fear. My pain is my strength, an invitation to journey within. It is a signal for me, a time of reflection and new choices. Pain opens the door to understanding.

Sometimes I feel that too much joy and success will bring an end to me. After all, it was only through suffering and pain that I felt alive. Then my passion for life kicks in, reminding me that I'm not ready to leave this journey. There's a dimension of me I have never touched, and maybe never will, at least not in this lifetime. This very mystery of life fuels me with the energy of living, loving and seeking truth.

I learned to stop blaming all the evil people in my life for what they have done to me. By taking responsibility for my involvement with these people in the first place, I could see that the anger in my adult life was coming from the hurt I had in my childhood. Understanding this anger was the missing link to my original pain. The wounded child inside of me, who believed she deserved the abuse, was filled with shame and self-hate. She was trying to validate her survivability. I could clearly see that she led me toward horrible situations just to prove she could survive. I set myself up for so much pain, so much abuse — my defenses could no longer protect me. Finally, the fear of where I was at was greater than the fear of where I wanted to go.

Only then could I feel my original pain. For the first time I was able to grieve. I realized that I was using all my strength in giving out energy, never getting anything back. No wonder I felt so weak. The reality is that I'm not a weak person at all — look what I survived as a child! If the kid in me was that strong, imagine how strong my adult was.

It was here I learned about choices. Something so simple and free as a choice was something I never knew. I realized that as an abused child I had taken ownership of the abuse rather than feel helpless. By owning the abuse as a child, it kept me helpless in my adult life. I had turned all the anger and rage in on myself. The anger I turned inward filled me with depression and shame, and kept me from knowing that I had any other choice but to suffer. Slowly but surely I got the negative energies out of my life. I learned to channel my inner strength by taking risks in safer, more productive places. Now when I give out energies, there is a higher probability that I'll receive energy back. Today I'm a successful professional speaker and therapist. But most important, I feel peace within.

WHAT IS ANGER?

Have you ever been angry? Have you ever been hurt by someone who has been angry with you? And, maybe just once, have you ever hurt someone else as a result of your anger? I am sure you can answer yes to at least one of these questions. Anger is a natural emotion people experience when they are feeling threatened or hurt. *It is always a secondary emotion.* This is a really important point to remember. Feeling threatened or hurt is the primary emotion you experience. Anger is the result of feeling threatened or hurt. Tracing down to the primary emotion shows you that anger is a choice.

Let's look at the following example: You are driving your car down the highway. Someone swerves in front of you, almost causing you to wreck. What happens? If you're like most people, you become angry at the person in the other car. You were almost killed! Your life was in danger! You have the right to be angry. But what was your first feeling? Was it anger? No. You were scared. You became angry only when the accident didn't happen, when you knew you were safe from harm.

This example shows how anger is a secondary emotion. Because anger is always a secondary emotion, you have time to choose how you are going to react to being threatened or hurt.

So the next time you find yourself getting angry, stop and ask yourself: What am I threatened or hurt about?

This exercise helps you see how you cannot be angry unless you have been hurt or scared. In the situation you described, was it worth the investment? It takes a lot of energy to use anger, so you want to use it wisely. What happens to many of us is that we skip over what we're really threatened about to hide our hurt under the disguise of anger. If I can intimidate you with my anger, you won't know I'm scared or hurt. We end up projecting our hurt onto others. By doing this, we never get rid of our pain.

What pain are you carrying inside of you?

_____

_____

_____

By tracing anger down, you will actually feel the hurt in your gut. Connecting with the hurt helps validate you and enables you to feel stronger, healthier anger. It grounds you. Having connected with your pain, the hurt will tell you if you want to invest in the anger phase. If you don't validate your hurt, your anger comes out in unmanageable ways. You then try to validate your pain by how hurt someone else becomes as a result of your anger. How can you know how mad you wish to be if you don't know how hurt you are? Anger is only bad if you hurt yourself or someone else because of it. Healthy anger is a way of saying no to abusive situations: "I am no longer a victim."

═══ DRAW A PICTURE OF YOUR ANGER

Draw a picture of what your anger looks like. Don't worry about artistic merit; draw from your heart.

WHO ARE YOU ANGRY WITH?

Make a list of the people you're angry
with. Describe how each of these people
have hurt you.

People I am angry with	How they hurt me
_____	_____
_____	_____
_____	_____
_____	_____
_____	_____
_____	_____
_____	_____

How Do You Express Your Anger?

How you behave as an adult when you become angry can come from the messages you received about anger as a child. You may have received some negative or painful messages about anger, and as an adult you may have special problems when it comes to this emotion. Let's say you came from a violent, abusive family, a family that screamed and hit. As an adult you may avoid anger because you've learned that anger hurts, that anger shames and destroys.

You may also be the type of person who lets a lot of people dump on you and never says a word. Then you may end up taking your anger out on the ones you love, the people you feel closest to. Why do you hurt the ones you love? Because the security in those relationships allows unlikable qualities in you to come up and show. Yes, you must really work on that because healthy loving relationships mean safety. They shouldn't be that much work.

Perhaps you came from a family that never expressed anger, and as an adult you feel angry all the time. Of course you would! Anger is a natural emotion. What did you do with your anger all those years you were growing up? You stored it up inside of you because you learned it was not okay to get mad and show your feelings.

Are some of these situations beginning to make sense to you? I hope so. You're not alone. So many of us have had problems with anger. So many of us have had our share of pain.

Most of us received negative messages about anger when we were children. Probably as adults we give out some negative

messages. Don't be too hard on yourself —
awareness is the key to change. All behaviors
have a meaning. But behaviors can be
changed — if you want to make the changes.

If you discover that you received negative
messages as a child, you cannot expect that
those negative messages will magically go
away simply because you grew up. Adults
are merely grown-up children.

THE INSIGHT QUESTIONNAIRE

The purpose of the Insight Questionnaire
is to help you reflect on the messages you
received about anger as a child. Those childhood anger messages govern your anger behavior as an adult.

Use the Insight Questionnaire to give
yourself a little bit of permission and self-
acceptance for your angry feelings. How you
behave when you are angry is probably a
result of what was taught to you about
anger as a child. Keep in mind that maybe
your anger behavior has a protective meaning for you, regardless of whether it is appropriate or not. When you understand why

you behave the way you do, it will be easier for you to make productive changes.

The Insight Questionnaire helps you to reflect on the past messages you received concerning anger. Once you understand how those messages influence your present behavior, you will be laying the necessary groundwork for constructive changes.

Now you are ready to begin the Insight Questionnaire.

Please answer the following questions as spontaneously as possible.

1. As a child when my mother became angry, she _____

_____

When my father became angry, he _____

_____

When my brother/sister/other became angry, _____

_____

2. I responded by:

____ Pouting   ____ Throwing things

_____ Avoiding   _____ Blaming others

_____ Crying   _____ Holding feelings in

           _____ Yelling

_____ Feeling sick   _____ Hiding

_____ Hitting   _____ Other

    3. As an adult, I express or show my anger by _____

_____

    4. Three situations that make me angry are:

      1. _____

      2. _____

      3. _____

      4. I react by _____

      5. I feel guilty when I express or show my anger by _____

_____

How did you do with this questionnaire? Are you beginning to see how messages you received as a child can affect your behavior as an adult? Did answering the questions bring up some emotions for you? Did you have some trouble remembering? If you did, that's okay. That's a message to you that anger may have been very painful for you as a child. For your own survival, you chose to block out those memories. Have compassion for yourself. The memories will come when you're safe enough to deal with them.

MAKING CHANGES

Let's say as a child, when you were around angry situations in your family, you were physically abused. You learned as a child that anger meant danger. As an adult you may over-react to anger by throwing things or hitting. The wounded child inside of you is pulling from past memories. When anger occurs in the present moment, you feel the need to protect yourself by physically acting out. The child in you becomes afraid. You protect this child by attacking the person you're angry with. Make sense? The adult is so caught up with the present, you may not realize you were acting out in the past. Throwing and hitting protect you from being hit. Actually this behavior only sets you up to be hurt. After all, when you hit people, they're probably going to hit you back.

When will you make changes? When you've had enough, and maybe not a minute sooner. When the fear of where you are is greater than the fear of where you want to go, then you will make changes. How sad that childhood abuse can enable adults to tolerate so much before they can let go.

What is keeping you from making changes? _____

_____

_____

_____

_____

One way I hide my angry feelings is by

_____

_____

_____

Sometimes I show my angry feelings by

_____

_____

_____

I think I'm beginning to understand

_____

_____

_____

═══ A WRITING EXERCISE

Get out a pen or pencil and some blank pages. For the next 20 minutes, without stopping your pen, write down what you remember as a child about anger/abuse. Remember to include all the senses. What did you see? What did you smell, hear, feel? Say whatever you want. Don't worry about punctuation, or editing yourself in any way. If you run out of things to say, repeat whatever your thoughts are. Just keep your pen moving. Okay, begin.

When you are done, go back and read what you have written.

How do you feel when you read over your writing? Did you go blank? Did you go to other places — that is, start daydreaming? Did you have physical symptoms — headache, shortness of breath, tightening in your jaw, shoulders or neck?

Take a deep, full breath and breathe into your pain. Relax your body as you exhale. Now, on another piece of paper, simply write about what you experienced while you were writing.

Remember: Have *compassion* for yourself, for the feelings you are experiencing. Don't beat yourself up for where you are at. Why continue your abuse? Accepting "where you are at" is the beginning of the process to get "where you want to go."

Body Signals: SOS

S ending out signals (SOS) is exactly what your body will do when it is overloaded with anger and pain. Your body has a memory all its own and can remember everything that you have ever experienced. You may not be conscious of the messages your body is giving you to clue you in on your pain. If the hurt in your life has been severe, the body acts as a bulletproof vest so the hurt does not destroy you. As a bulletproof vest stops bullets, your body absorbs pain.

As a child you learned to armor yourself when abuse occurred. Your body began holding in the pain because this was safer than feeling the pain. In this way the wounded child's ability to feel is lessened. When the body holds the pain, the child learns to numb out emotionally. The problem really begins when the child becomes an adult and sets up intense situations just to feel. As you become emotionally safer in your adult life, your body will really start talking to you because it no longer has to hold the pain.

When you experience anger in your body, your heart rate increases, your pupils dilate, blood sugar and blood pressure go up, adrenaline flows (this is what feels scary), the pituitary gland increases secretions, digestion and elimination slow down, breathing rate goes up, blood vessels constrict, and muscles contract.

If all this happens when you get angry and block feelings, imagine what happens to your body if you hold in feelings over a period of years. The body responds to the suppressed anger with somatic symptoms such as skin rashes, ulcers, allergies, TMJ (jaw tightness), gastrointestinal problems, head-aches, backaches, chronic fatigue (depression), insomnia, ear aches, and so on. If you are not in touch with your original pain, start listening to the SOS. It can be your key to healing.

When you were a child victim, your body learned early in life to numb your pain. As an adult you may be unaware of the tightness and aches in your muscles. This tightness prevents the flow of feelings, causing you physical symptoms. Have you ever said, "Oh, my neck hurts. I must have slept on it the wrong way?" I assure you that it wasn't just that you slept on it wrong; it was your body responding to unconscious pain. You may wake up feeling stiff or clenching your jaws. The tightening of jaws is especially connected to anger issues.

As an adult child you are certain to have fear issues. When you become afraid, you stop breathing. So if you've had a lot of fear issues, begin to notice how you breathe. If you are a shallow breather, make a conscious attempt to breathe deeper. Not taking in deep breaths over a long period of time can cause tightness in the neck and shoulders.

So breathe. Inhale, take in life. Exhale, and let go of fear!

The very nature of breathing creates safety so you can get in touch with your feelings.

SOS Messages

What SOS messages can you hear? What physical symptoms do you experience? ____

_____

_____

_____

_____

_____

DEFENSES

We develop our defenses at a very early age. They protect us from whatever is going on in our environment. There is nothing wrong with these defenses if they helped us survive the abuse. The problem begins in adulthood, when these same defenses that once protected us keep us from having safe, loving, intimate relationships as adults.

As a little one, you are innocent. What could a little one do that could be so horrible? You did not deserve abusive treatment, but you have taken ownership of your abuse rather than be helpless.

If you are still acting out abusively as an adult, yes, you must take responsibility for your actions. This is an absolute. Healing as an adult, regardless of what happened to you as a little one, means you must take responsibility for healthy living. This may not seem fair. But to truly uncover and recover, you must stop rationalizing at the expense of yourself or others.

It doesn't seem fair that you have to pay for therapists, workshops, books and tapes. It makes you feel that you're still a victim. Do it anyway! It will stop you from passing on abusive patterns to others and bring true joy into your life.

The rewards you received from your suffering will bring you many gifts of enlightenment. As you begin to experience inner peace, you will realize that getting help is not about being a victim at all. It is about fighting back and taking action.

Human beings are dependent on one another. Babies would not survive without a lifeline. You depend on a mechanic when your car breaks down. If you break your arm, you are dependent on a doctor. Dependent relationships will only be a problem to you if they are based on unhealthy dependencies. Healthy dependencies enable us to thrive and take productive risks. Defenses include:

- Denial — blocking out painful realities
- Projection — placing your feelings on someone else
- Repression — numbing out feelings
- Dissociation — "leaving your body" when the trauma is so great or terrifying that you need an instant form of numbing
- Displacement — placing your pain somewhere else
- Identification — when victim identifies with offender
- Conversion — to compensate for abuse you convert your feelings into other thoughts, feelings or behaviors
- Minimizing — discounting abuse

- Reaction formation — doing just the opposite of what was done to you
- Overcompensation — covering up insecurities by overemphasis on some other characteristic
- Rationalization — making excuses
- Emotional insulation — emotionally withdrawing to reduce involvement

THINKING ABOUT YOUR DEFENSES

What defenses have you used?

_____

_____

_____

_____

_____

ANGER STUDY

Please answer the following questions as honestly as possible. Use the anger study to evaluate where you are with anger.

1. When I get angry, the feeling I experience:
   - ☐ threatens me   ☐ weakens me
   - ☐ is very intense   ☐ feels natural

2. I would consider myself to be:
   - ☐ a very angry aggressive person
   - ☐ about average as an angry person
   - ☐ a very passive person

3. Sometimes, I communicate my anger by:
   - ☐ name calling
   - ☐ yelling
   - ☐ displaying anger in public view
   - ☐ using swear words
   - ☐ bringing up past issues
   - ☐ throwing things
   - ☐ other

4. I suffer from:
   - ☐ over or undereating
   - ☐ frequent headaches
   - ☐ back pain
   - ☐ ulcers
   - ☐ grinding teeth
   - ☐ anxiety attacks
   - ☐ depression
   - ☐ asthma or allergies
   - ☐ constipation — diarrhea
   - ☐ other

5. The behavior that most describes how I deal with anger is:
   - ☐ nagging
   - ☐ avoiding
   - ☐ angry outbursts
   - ☐ humor
   - ☐ sarcasm
   - ☐ open expression
   - ☐ emotional problems
   - ☐ in-out relationships
   - ☐ drinking — drugs
   - ☐ other

6. Sometimes, I express anger indirectly by:
   □ gossiping   □ finding fault
   □ driving too fast   □ bitterness
   □ taking anger out   □ blaming others
      on my children   □ other

7. Some situations that influence my getting angry are:
   □ financial pressure   □ past experiences
   □ loss of sleep   □ in-law troubles
   □ family dynamics   □ jealousy
   □ insecurity   □ being late
   □ trouble at work   □ mood swings
   □ poor self-image   □ laid off or fired
   □ increased working   from work
      hours   □ other

8. Frequently I find myself angry toward:
   □ my children   □ my friends
   □ my mate   □ my co-workers
   □ strangers   □ other
   □ my boss

9. I become angry at myself when I:
   □ worry about what others think of me
   □ have to be in large groups of people
   □ have bad dreams
   □ feel inferior to others
   □ can't make decisions

10. The person or people I am most angry
    with are: _____
    _____
    _____
    _____

Is Your Anger Healthy?

Our society is obsessed with behavior in everyday living and determining whether the behavior is healthy, unhealthy, appropriate or inappropriate. Some of us think that having a normal life means having a life without problems. This just isn't so. Life presents us with problems. That's natural — it's called reality. Remember, if there is no stress involved, it may not be worth doing.

How we respond to problems is what makes people different. But because life doesn't always present us with easy problems, we sometimes feel that we aren't adequately prepared to cope with our problems and the people who present them.

Anger is a complex, intense emotion. Anger is unhealthy when you hurt yourself or others because of your angry feelings. Keep in mind that anger turned inward is called depression. Anger that hurts others is called destructive.

All human beings get angry. How you behave when you become angry determines whether your anger is healthy or unhealthy.

Here are some suggestions to find out if your anger is getting the best of you:

- If you find yourself having negative thoughts or frequent anger outbursts.
- If you experience frequent anxiety or panic attacks.
- If you're depressed often or for long periods at a time.
- If you are an aggressive person — your anger allows you to hurt others to get what you want.

• If you are a passive person — the anger you hold in allows other people to hurt you.

IRRITABILITY INDICATOR

Measure your *Irritability Level* by reading the list of twenty potentially stressful situations. In the space besides each situation, estimate the degree it would anger or upset you, using this simple rating scale.

0 = I would feel very little or no anger.
1 = I would feel a little angry or upset.
2 = I would feel moderately angry.
3 = I would feel very angry.
4 = I would feel extremely angry.

_____ 1. While carrying groceries into your house, the bag breaks, spilling the groceries all over the sidewalk.

_____ 2. You plug in your new toaster and it doesn't work.

_____ 3. Someone makes a mistake and blames it on you.

_____ 4. Your boss reprimands you for something while the actions of others go unnoticed.

____ 5. You get a flat tire on the way to work.

____ 6. You have a 1:00 appointment with your dentist, and you are not seen until 3:15.

____ 7. You are being ignored.

____ 8. You make plans to go somewhere, but the person backs out at the last moment.

____ 9. You are trying to read, but someone near you keeps talking to you.

____ 10. Your car stalls at a traffic light, and the guy behind you keeps blowing his horn.

____ 11. Someone knocks a stack of important papers out of your hand, but fails to help you pick them up.

____ 12. You are shopping and the salesclerk won't leave you alone.

____ 13. You are trying to express your feelings to someone who will not listen.

____ 14. You are in a hurry, but the car in front of you is going under the speed limit.

_____ 15. Your best friend asks your new romance to a party, but fails to invite you.

_____ 16. You lend a friend something of value to you, and the friend fails to return it.

_____ 17. You step on a wad of bubble gum.

_____ 18. You did not get the promotion you asked for.

_____ 19. Your friend calls you at 1:00 a.m. to tell you he can't sleep.

_____ 20. You receive your doctor bill and feel you have been overcharged.

Now interpret your total score according to the following scale:

A score between 45 and 68 indicates that your anger behavior is within a normal range. However, you may not be pleased with your overall behavior and may want to change parts of your anger behavior.

A score between 0 and 44 or between 69 and 80 indicates that you need to work on your anger. The fact that you are completing the exercises says you're interested in changing your behavior. You deserve a pat on the

back. But if you find the exercises included
aren't working, seek professional help.

0 – 36   The amount of irritability you usu-
         ally experience is remarkably low.
         Only a small percent of the popula-
         tion score this low on the indicator.
         A score this low may mean that you
         are holding your anger inside. You
         may experience stomach cramps or
         muscle spasms when you are angry.

37 – 44 You are considerably more passive
         than the average person. Don't get
         me wrong, this does not mean that
         you are not angry. Again, passive
         people hold their anger inside.

45 – 60 You react to life's stresses with an
         average amount of anger.

61 – 68 You experience anger often and re-
         spond to life's stresses with more
         irritation than the average person.

69 – 80 You are an intense person and have
         frequent anger outbursts that do
         not quickly disappear. You may have
         the reputation of hothead among
         people who know you. Your anger
         may get you into trouble in your
         professional and private worlds.

You may experience headaches and high blood pressure. Only a small percent of the population react as intensely to stress as you do.

If you scored very low, suggesting you are passive, yet you feel very angry inside, you're probably saying, "This doesn't fit me." Remember, the passive person is the angry person who holds anger in and lets other people dump on them.

If you scored average, it simply means you're healthy with your anger, you express your anger as you feel it.

If your score is very high, this may suggest you are a person who carries anger inside. You over-invest in irritating situations so that past feelings can come up for some temporary relief. This score suggests that you're sitting on some painful memories. You may need additional support to get to the root of your problem. See Appendix A for suggestions.

Perhaps you feel like an angry person but didn't invest in any of these situations listed on the indicator. This could suggest that you are experiencing intense stress in your present life, such as divorce, sexual harassment at work, career change, moving or loss of job. The questions on the indicator seem mild to what you're going through at the moment. All changes revolve around a loss of some sort.

ACTING OUT ANGER

These are ways we act out anger:

- Blaming others: It seems safer to focus on someone else rather than yourself.
- Pouting: You play out the silent treatment because you're in the hurt phase of anger.
- Throwing things: You very quickly want to skip over the part of you that is hurt or threatened, to get further and further away from your hurt.
- Avoiding anger: It has not been safe for you to express anger. The repercussions have been severe.
- Feeling sick: This comes from holding the intensity of anger in, creating a nauseating experience.
- Guilt: This is a learned way out of making a decision.

Which ones apply to you? How do you feel about that? _____

_____

_____

==== **STRESSORS I WANT TO ELIMINATE**

This is a list of sources of stress that can lead to conflict and violence. Check the stressors you are currently experiencing.

1. Troubles with the boss
2. Troubles with other people at work
3. Laid off or fired from work
4. Arrested or convicted on some serious charge.
5. Death of someone close
6. Foreclosure of mortgage or loan
7. Pregnancy or childbirth
8. Serious illness or injury
9. Serious problems with health or behavior of a family member
10. Sexual difficulties
11. In-law troubles
12. Much worse off financially
13. Separated or divorced

14. Big increase in number of arguments with spouse or partner
15. Big increase in hours of work or job responsibility
16. Moving to a different neighborhood or town
17. Child kicked out of school
18. Child caught doing something illegal

Now prioritize your stressors according to which brings you the most discomfort. Which one do you want to work on first, second, third, and so on? When you look at all your stressors at once, you get overwhelmed and take no action. It doesn't matter how emotionally or mentally strong you are, if you are having multiple stressors in your life, expect some emotional or behavioral change.

1. _____
2. _____
3. _____
4. _____
5. _____
6. _____

7. _____

8. _____

9. _____

10. _____

What Keeps You From Expressing Anger?

During my seminars I ask people, "What keeps you from expressing anger?" I obtain many answers that I've come to call barriers. Below is a list of some of the more common barriers people have experienced. These barriers keep them from expressing their anger. For those people (and maybe even you) these barriers are very real. But once you examine your individual barriers — get them out in the open — you can overcome them. Do the thing you fear the most, and that will be the death of fear.

1. **Low self-esteem.** Self-esteem is the mental picture you have of yourself. It is what you think and how you feel about yourself. When you like yourself, you simply won't let people treat you badly.

2. **Fear of losing control.** If you tell yourself you will lose control, you will lose control. Worry is believing in negative things. Your emotions don't control you, you control your emotions.

3. **Fear of appearing weak.** You may have learned as a child that expressing your feelings shows weakness. As a child you may have told someone how you felt, and then you were taken advantage of. Perhaps your innocence opened you up to being hurt by others. Expressing honest anger is never a sign of weakness, but a sign of strength. People who do not let you know how they feel are weak.

4. **Fear of rejection.** Rejection-avoidance behavior governs more of our behavior than any single factor. Keep in mind

that the anticipation of rejection is far worse than the actual rejection.

5. **Fear of retaliation.** Anger is only harmful when you hurt another person. When you express honest anger without attacking the other person, there is no reason for retaliation.

6. **Fear of hurting the other person's feelings.** It is a full-time job being responsible for your own feelings. Worrying about other people's feelings is a way of avoiding your own.

RULES FOR EXPRESSING ANGER

1. Breathe into your anger and validate your hurt or threat. Exhale deeply.
2. Make a conscious choice. Is the hurt worth investing in anger?
3. Select a private, safe setting should you choose to invest in the anger.
4. If possible, go directly to the person you are angry with.
5. Tell yourself to be prepared to listen.
6. Stick to the issues.
7. Practice direct eye contact.
8. State how you feel.

Let's take a few minutes to review each rule in more detail.

1. **Breathe into your anger.** Breathing creates safety so that you can feel what is hurting or threatening you.
2. **Make a conscious choice.** Connecting with the hurt or fear enables you to manage anger. It keeps you from over- or under-investing.
3. **Select a private setting.** If possible, find a private place where you and the other person can be alone. This private setting shows that you respect yourself and the other person.
4. **Go directly to the person you are angry with.** Try to be as direct as possible. If you are angry with someone, it may help to discuss the situation with an objective person for another point of view. But you will get better results if you go directly to the person you are angry with.
5. **Be prepared to listen.** This relates to the fourth rule. If you are so angry that you cannot hear the other person, wait until you are ready to listen, then find

that other person. Eighty percent of all communication is spent on listening.

6. **Stick to the issue.** Go back and ask yourself what you are threatened or hurt about. Then address that issue. If that issue is valid, give yourself permission to be angry, but stick to that issue when expressing your anger.

7. **Practice direct eye contact.** This can be difficult. Direct eye contact means you are serious. When you don't look at the other person, he or she feels discounted. However, direct eye contact does not mean staring the other person down.

8. **State how you feel.** Use "I feel . . ." statements at all times. "You make me . . ." statements threaten the other person and put that person on the defensive. A person who feels defensive will fight back.

EXPRESSING ANGER APPROPRIATELY

Rules provide you with structure. Try to remember that anger is simply another feeling that needs to be communicated — you are not at war with that person. But it often feels that way. Why? Because you're trying to get the person you're angry with to validate your feelings, to tell you it's okay to be mad. What's important is that *you* validate your own feelings of anger, and then communicate your feelings to the person you're angry with. If you wait for other people to give you permission to be angry, you may be waiting a long time.

What's keeping you from expressing your anger appropriately? _____

_____

_____

_____

INDIRECT EXPRESSIONS OF ANGER

When anger is not expressed directly, it comes out indirectly. I've included a diagram called *Indirect Expressions of Anger*, which may help you understand that the people around you are also having difficulty expressing anger.

INDIRECT METHODS OF EXPRESSING ANGER

HOLDING IN

Self-criticism
Guilt
Depression
Bitterness

INDIRECT

Nagging
Gossiping
Sarcasm
Displacing
Withdrawing

VIOLENCE

FOCUSING OUTSIDE
SELF

Blaming Others
Finding Fault
Angry Outbursts

ACTING OUT

Stealing
Drinking
Drugs
Driving too fast
Affairs

TO SELF

Psychosomatic
problems

TO OTHERS

Physical Abuse

Murder

Suicide

Were you surprised to see so many disguises of anger? Let me add a few more to your list:

- **Impatience** — These people expect the world to meet their needs. They are often angry because of being let down by others.
- **Prejudice** — What else could prejudice be, other than an indirect way of letting anger out. There just isn't any other explanation for it.
- **Procrastination** — Think of the angry self-talk you give yourself when you put off doing something.
- **Being late** — What a power trip. You make your grand entrance and everyone is mad at you! What a set-up!

=== **MISPLACING ANGER**

The mind knows that in order for the body to be healthy, feelings must come out. If you are not in touch with your feelings, your mind will search for "reasons" so that you can be angry and avoid your true sense of hurt. The problem with indirect anger is you wind up turning the anger back in on yourself because these angry situations aren't your real issues.

Where do you misplace your anger? _____

_____

_____

_____

_____

Angry feelings have to come out. Think of that stored-up anger inside of you, looking to get out. Take some time to go back and study the indirect expressions of anger.

How many of these behaviors apply to you or someone you know? _____

_____

_____

_____

_____

My Behavior	**Others**
_____	_____
_____	_____
_____	_____
_____	_____

What Is An Anger Action Plan?

An Anger Action Plan is an outline of actions that helps you make behavioral changes. The Anger Action Plan helps you learn to control specific parts of your behavior. As Benjamin Disraeli said, "Action may not always bring happiness, but without action, there is no happiness."

In Chapter 8 you will plan what you'll do daily to work on changing your anger behavior by using this step-by-step procedure.

Sound complicated? Not really. You've already learned a great deal about your anger behavior. By now you know . . .

- what anger is and where it comes from
- how your childhood feelings about anger affect your adult life
- what happens to your body
- your anger level
- some barriers that others have stated for expressing anger
- defenses

SELF-ESTEEM

Self-esteem is the mental picture you have of yourself — what you think and feel about yourself. Who is responsible for your self-esteem? You are! But how many times do you look for someone else to make you happy? Until you are comfortable with yourself, you will not be happy with anyone else.

You may be asking, "Can I change my self-image? Can I learn to feel good about myself?" The answer is yes. But first you must change your negative thinking and develop a positive mind.

How does one stop thinking negatively? First, you stop spending time dwelling on your weaknesses: I'm too fat, not smart enough, and so on. Sound familiar? When you spend time thinking about your weak areas, you will not have any energy left to work on them. Each day look in the mirror and say 10 good statements about yourself. If you can't convince the person in the mirror, you can't convince anyone else. Invest in your strengths and begin believing in yourself.

Stop holding on to past failures. When you spend time thinking and feeling bad about what you can no longer change, you become stuck in the past. Don't run away from yourself. Yes, it hurts to look at your past and the mistakes you have made, but you will hurt a lifetime when you run away from yourself.

Self-esteem is power. It is the highest source of power you will ever achieve. Once you have it, no one can ever take it away from you. You own it. It belongs to you. Take a chance on yourself and begin to live.

Take the self-esteem quiz. When you finish scoring, circle the areas you wish to work on. After you finish the quiz, go back and focus on your strong areas. Begin this process by writing down 10 good things you like about yourself.

SELF-ESTEEM QUIZ

Please answer the following questions with a yes or a no.

_____ 1. Are you often concerned about what other people think of you?

_____ 2. Are you able to communicate your real feelings?

_____ 3. Do you often wish your life could have been different?

_____ 4. Do you judge your self-worth by comparing yourself to others?

_____ 5. Are you free of emotional turmoil and guilt?

_____ 6. Do large crowds threaten you?

_____ 7. Do you make your own decisions?

_____ 8. Do you often criticize others?

_____ 9. Do you tend to put yourself down?

_____ 10. Can you recognize your strong points?

_____ 11. Can you freely express anger?

_____ 12. Do you often feel inferior to others?

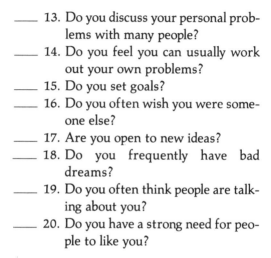

____ 13. Do you discuss your personal problems with many people?

____ 14. Do you feel you can usually work out your own problems?

____ 15. Do you set goals?

____ 16. Do you often wish you were someone else?

____ 17. Are you open to new ideas?

____ 18. Do you frequently have bad dreams?

____ 19. Do you often think people are talking about you?

____ 20. Do you have a strong need for people to like you?

ANSWERS:

1. No; 2. Yes; 3. No; 4. No; 5. Yes; 6. No; 7. Yes; 8. No; 9. No; 10. Yes; 11. Yes; 12. No; 13. No; 14. Yes; 15. Yes; 16. No; 17. Yes; 18. No; 19. No; 20. No.

SCORING: Give yourself one point for each right answer.

16 to 20 points: You are an exceptionally secure person with high self-esteem.

6 to 15 points: You are confident in most situations and fearful of few. You have a good self-image most of the time. However, in some areas you could work on improvements.

1 to 5 points: Your self-image could use improvement. Spend less time thinking of your weaknesses and more time focusing on your strengths. Awareness is the key to change. Take action!

10 Good Things I Like About Myself Are:

1. _____
2. _____
3. _____
4. _____
5. _____
6. _____
7. _____

8. _____

9. _____

10. _____

ANGER ASSESSMENT QUESTIONNAIRE

The changes we make in life largely depend on what we really feel inside. This questionnaire provides you with an opportunity to see in black and white the silent feelings you have within.

1. What am I currently doing about expressing honest anger that makes me feel better about myself?

   a. reading this workbook

   _____

   _____

   _____

2. What do I consider a "not worthwhile" behavior concerning my anger?

   _____

   _____

   _____

3. What do I fear the most about expressing my anger?

   _____

   _____

4. What would make me feel better about my ability to express anger?

_____

_____

5. Starting tomorrow, I would like to change my approach to anger by doing . . .

_____

_____

Your Personal Anger Action Plan

So now you're ready to begin your personal Anger Action Plan. Taking time to sign and date your action plan validates your commitment to change. What's the difference between thinking about making a change and making a change? *Action!*

I pledge to work on my anger issues with this Plan, which I have created myself.

Signed: _____

Date: _____

PERSONAL ANGER

In the space below, make a list of situations that make you angry in your personal life.

1. _____
2. _____
3. _____
4. _____

PRIORITIZE YOUR SITUATIONS

Which situation do you want to eliminate first, second, third and so on?

1. _____
2. _____
3. _____
4. _____

BARRIERS

Now list your barriers (what keeps you from expressing anger) in the situations you have just listed.

_____

_____

_____

_____

_____

══ TAKING ACTION

Now list what action steps you can take to overcome those barriers. See "Anger Assessment Questionnaire" for ideas. Use positive action statements.

1. _____

2. _____

3. _____

4. _____

══ DAILY "ANGER" ACTION PLANS

List what actions you will take on a daily basis to help you express honest anger. Refer to rules.

1. _____

2. _____

3. _____

4. _____

REWARDS

You need positive reinforcement once you've achieved one of your action steps. It is important to reward yourself so that you will have an incentive to continue your positive approach to anger.

The Difference Between Thinking About
A Change And Making That Change
IS ACTION

Now list the rewards you will receive as you overcome your barriers.

Example: Attend a motivational seminar on

self-esteem.

_____

_____

_____

_____

_____

_____

APPENDIX: GUIDELINES FOR SEEKING SUPPORT

1. Make sure you feel a comfortable energy with whomever you choose to do your work with.
2. See if a friend you trust could refer a professional to you.
3. Make sure you feel safe in the physical environment. Do you like the pictures in the office? The furniture? Those physical characteristics can tell you a lot about that person.
4. What is the fee? Is there a sliding scale fee? Ask! It is always okay to ask questions.
5. Does this person treat you like an equal?
6. Do you feel good around this person? Don't give up your power if you feel insecure or threatened by this per-

son. Choose someone else. You may have to search before you find the person for you. So many people stay in relationships that are not healthy for them and never say a word! Don't worry about hurting their feelings! Just because someone has credentials doesn't mean he or she is healthy. You do have choices.

7. Is the therapist strong enough to confront your issues?

8. If it is a seminar you plan to attend, is it cost effective for you? Find out what objectives will be covered. Do they fit your needs?

9. Is the seminar leader someone with a good reputation? Do you know anyone else who has attended?

10. Ask what materials will be given to you. Call the seminar leader and talk with him or her.

11. Don't just rush into every program that comes into your area. It may be a waste of time and money.

HEAR DEVON WEBER!

Devon Weber is a nationally known speaker and consultant specializing in Anger Recovery. By drawing heavily upon her personal experiences as a survivor of incest and severe childhood abuse, Devon's workshops are particularly powerful.

WORKSHOPS

The Anger Connection — The Missing Link to Recovery — The Making of an Angry Child — Surviving Childhood Sexual Abuse, Anger and Co-dependency — Clues to Original Pain, Feelings, Anger — The Adult Child in the Workplace — Anger: The Backbone of Healing — The Art of Saying No — Letting Go of Anger, Fear and Depression

Devon's training and extensive background in the mental health field, creatively blended with her life experiences, make her a talented and gifted professional. She is former Co-ordinator and Director of an Adult Psychiatric Program, Co-founder of New Visions Psychological Services, author of *Angry? Do You Mind If I Scream?* and president of Inner Dynamics Consulting. Devon has recently appeared on the *Sally Jessy Raphael* show, as well as *Donahue* and *Geraldo*.

Anger Is Your Choice: A Cassette Program with Handbook is also available for $15.95 plus $2.50 for postage and handling.

If you are interested in having Devon conduct a lecture or workshop for your group, learn when she may be speaking in your area, or wish to order *Anger Is Your Choice*, contact:

John E. Hunger
INFINITY PRESS
6705 N. Lamar, #245
Austin, TX 78752
512-458-9890 or 800-477-8398